SAVE O

CAUSING A
Stink!

The
Eco Warrior's
Handbook

CAROLINE CLAYTON

FRIENDS *of the* earth

All About Friends of the Earth

Friends of the Earth was set up in 1971 and now has around 200,000 supporters working together to help protect the environment. There are 250 local groups around England, Wales and Northern Ireland and it is the largest environmental network in the world with groups in 50 countries around the world, from Scotland to New Zealand and Latvia to the Philippines.

Every year Friends of the Earth adds new successes to its list, saving more and more important wildlife sites and helping to protect endangered plants and animals.

Join us in:

- **protecting homes for animals and plants**
- **stopping the destruction of tropical rainforests**
- **preventing pollution of air, water and land**
- **cutting down on waste and encouraging reuse and recycling**
- **promoting a more sustainable way of living – looking after the environment and our planet makes life better for people too**

Plus much, much more.

Friends of the Earth
26-28 Underwood Street
London N1 7JQ
Telephone 0171 490 1555
Email: info@foe.co.uk

Many thanks to Sarah Finch, Athena Lamnisos, Tabby Patterson,
Sue Meagher, Neil Verlander, Sarah Welsh, Mary Taylor,
Pad Green, Roger Higman, Duncan McLaren, Anna Stanford,
Tim Rice, Alan Watson and Mike Clowes for all their help.

First published in Great Britain in 1996
Bloomsbury Publishing Plc, 2 Soho Square, London W1V 6HB

Copyright © Friends of the Earth

The moral rights of the author and illustrator have been asserted
A CIP catalogue record for this book
is available from the British Library

ISBN 0 7475 2685 0

Printed by Cox and Wyman, Reading, Berkshire

10 9 8 7 6 5 4 3 2 1

Chapter One

STICK YOUR PHOTO HERE

PERSONAL FILE

Name

_____

Affectionately known as

_____

Age

_____ years_____months

The rest of this chapter must be filled in by the owner of this book. If this book doesn't belong to you, stop reading now and return it to its rightful owner. The following details are TOP SECRET!

My number one pal is

_____

and my other best friends are

_____

_____

and

_____

My claim to fame

_____

_____

Grooviest item in my wardrobe

_____

_____

My pets

_____

_____

_____

My hero/heroine

_____

_____

_____

One thing I'd ban to make life better

_____

_____

_____

If I were an animal I'd like to be a...

_____

_____

The best nature documentary I've ever seen

_____

Wild places I love

_____

_____

_____

Things that make me sad

_____

_____

Things that make me mad

_____

_____

and things that really spook me!

_____

_____

What I'd do if I were Prime Minister for a day

_____

_____

Clubs/organisations I belong to

_____

_____

I like reading books about

_____

_____

My favourite subject at school

_____

_____

My silliest excuse for handing in late homework

_____

_____

Best swop I've ever made

_____

My favourite smell

_____

My favourite pizza topping

_____

_____

The daftest thing my dad/mum/brother/sister says to me

_____

_____

The job I'd most like to do when I'm older

_____

My best ever holiday (and why)

_____

_____

My favourite biscuit

_____

My star sign

_____

Personal best score on a computer game

_____

If I were a millionaire I'd

_____

_____

My most secret confession is

_____

_____

Chapter two

YOU CAN MAKE A DIFFERENCE!

Mayday! Mayday! Calling all eco warriors. This is an emergency! Planet Earth is under attack. And she can't fight back without your help.

It's serious. In the UK today, one in seven children has asthma. (If you live in a city area, one out of every three of your friends probably uses an inhaler.) You

can actually see the damage caused by acid rain on a quarter of all our trees. It's not safe to swim in the sea in some places.

Yet, until relatively recently things were quite different.

Ever since life began on Earth about 3 billion years ago, our environment has been changing. But these changes are speeding up. That's because more damage has been done to the planet in the last few centuries than at any other time in history.

Turn the page and take a look at what has happened in the last 100 years alone.

WHAT A DIFFERENCE 100 YEARS MAKES!

Life has changed in the UK since the beginning of this century. Today millions of folk are better off. But what's the point in living longer if you're destroying the planet?

In 1900, when Queen Victoria ruled, there were about 39 million people in Great Britain. Today there's a whopping 57 million and by the year 2000, according to United Nations, there will be over 6 billion people in the world – and nearly half of them will be under 20!

In 1900 there were so few cars on the UK roads that exhaust fumes weren't a problem. Most people travelled around in horse-drawn carriages. Yet today the average speed of a car in town is the same as that of a horse-drawn carriage because there are 24 million cars choking our roads. In 1900, extinction was a new concept. Now 50 species a day are dying out due to rainforest destruction.

In the last 50 years

...about one half of the world's rainforests have disappeared.

...ancient statues have become more damaged than they have over the previous 2000 years!

...we've used as much coal as in the whole of history to date.

...almost 50 per cent of Britain's ancient woodlands have been destroyed.

> *In 1971, a London survey found eight out of ten seven and eight-year-olds made their own way to school. Today, fewer than one in ten children travel without adult supervision. So children today have much less time hanging out with their mates, having fun and most importantly, learning to be independent, self-reliant people.*

The world needs eco warriors like you, now more than ever, because...

- a quarter of the world's species could become extinct in the next 20-30 years.

- our fossil fuels look set to run out soon. Only coal will last much beyond the end of the next century.

- other resources are running out too. For example eight out of the world's 17 ocean fisheries are being over-fished. That means that the fish populations in these water can't grow quickly enough to replace the ones being caught. These fish have had their chips!

When faced with problems on such a global scale it's hard to see how our own personal actions *can* make much difference. But individuals can change the world.

Using public transport, recycling our rubbish and buying greener products helps reduce our own personal impact on the world. It also encourages industry to be cleaner. However, the fate of the planet can't solely be left to individual action. Governments and companies have the biggest role to play. So as well as doing your bit, the eco warrior must put pressure on those with the power to help.

If you want to make a brighter future for the world, you've got to press for changes now. You may be the last generation who can stop the rot.

And if you're still not sure whether children can take on the world, read on. Over the page you can read about three eco warriors who are ringing the changes:

• **Nine-year-old James Silk** from Oxford stopped a 1000-year-old hedge from being bulldozed to make way for a new cricket pitch. James found that a lot of different animals living in the ancient hedgerow would lose their homes if it was cut down. So he persuaded a local planning inquiry to save the hedge. James's eco-victory will protect it for future generations.

• **13-year-old Debbie Simmons** is an old hand at green campaigning. For the last three years she has been on an advisory panel for her local zoo, Drusilla's Park in Eastbourne. In October 1995, they organised the first ever Children's International Environment Conference. Kids came from around the world to talk about the planet's problems.

"We felt that children's opinions were not being listened to and that adults weren't taking enough action to solve the problems themselves," Debbie says.

The conference has already had an effect. A local recycling centre was mightily impressed with the ideas the children came up with. So it has set up its own junior advisory board to generate more brilliant ideas.

• **15-year-old Justin Skelton** from Cornwall is a member of *Surfers against Sewage*. He and three other ace surfers are taking South West Water to court to stop them pumping raw sewage into the sea.

"They must treat the sewage properly and make it safe for people to swim", explains Justin. *"I know quite a few people who've been ill from surfing in this pollution. I had a week off school with a painful ear infection. When I went in the water again it came straight back."*

Justin believes it is especially important that young people try to stop adults messing up our planet.

"After all, we'll have to live with the problems they've created for a lot longer than they will. And that's not fair!"

Chapter three

HOW TO TAKE ON THE WORLD

Okay, so now you know that the planet needs your help. The thing is, just how do you get the world to take you seriously? Well, this won't be as difficult as you might think. Important people **will** take notice of you if you feel strongly about something. When lots of people feel the same way they can sway decisions made by local and national government.

Have you ever heard the saying 'It's not what you know, it's who you know'? If you want to take on the world, the recipe for success is knowing who makes decisions and who can change things for the better.

WHO CARES ABOUT THE PLANET?

This chart shows who makes decisions that affect the environment, on a local, national and global scale

LOCAL DECISIONS

Councils are responsible for looking after your local environment. They must take away household waste, monitor pollution and look after local transport. They also have a big say in the way land and open space is used around you.

Councils put national policy into practice. For example, the Government has declared that a quarter of all household rubbish must be recycled by the year 2000. Now it's up to councils to make sure this happens.

HOW THEY WORK:

In most places there are two local councils: county and district councils. But in and around large cities the council operates as one body. Whatever, all councils are split up into different departments eg Environmental Health, Planning, Housing etc.

Councils are made up of councillors and officers. **Councillors** are members voted for in local elections and are unpaid. They take the major decisions about council policy. **Officers** are the paid staff of the council. They do most of the day-to-day work.

NATIONAL DECISIONS

The Government makes the decisions which affect our environment - for better or sometimes for worse! It makes laws, adjusts taxes to encourage, or discourage, particular types of activities (for example, making petrol more expensive to encourage people to drive less), and pays for research into methods of pollution control.

HOW IT WORKS:

The Government consists of the Prime Minister, other Ministers responsible for particular areas such as Environment or Transport, and MPs (members of Parliament) who represent their 'constituencies' – local areas – as well as the party to which they belong.

GLOBAL DECISIONS

A lot of environmental problems are so big and wide-ranging that only an international effort can solve them. Unfortunately there's no effective international body to do this.

HOW IT WORKS:

The UK is one of 15 countries that belong to the European Union, or EU for short. The EU makes laws which each member country must stick to. Thanks to the EU, our Government has had to adopt stricter laws concerning pollution.

Sometimes governments from around the world get together to talk about important international issues and decide what needs to be done. For example, the decisions to ban commercial whaling and to cut ozone-destroying pollution were made this way. Unfortunately some countries tend to ignore international agreements if it suits them.

THE MEDIA

The power of newspapers, radio and TV can help bring about changes in public opinion and government policy. The media can make a small story big news within hours!

Now you know who to target, let's talk about tactics... and first, **a little about letter writing.**

Writing a letter to people in power is the easiest way to make a protest. For the best results follow our top ten letter writing tips, opposite.

ALL TOGETHER NOW

Although many people often feel strongly about something, very few actually bother to write a letter about it. It's thought that each person who puts pen to paper represents at least ten others who feel the same way.

Sometimes decision makers will only act if they receive hundreds, or thousands, of letters from the public. So always encourage others to write too. Or organise a petition.

Ten top letter writing tips

1) Always ask for an answer.
2) Explain clearly and briefly what you are concerned about...
3) ...include some facts and brief background information
4) ...then spell out what you want the reader to do about it.
5) Be polite!
6) If you don't know the name of the person you're writing to, start off with 'Dear Sir/Madam' and sign it 'Yours Faithfully'.
7) Use your best handwriting. Or better still type your letter...
8) ...and don't forget to include your age!
9) If you don't get a reply within ten days, phone to check that they got your letter. If you still don't get a reply, write a reminder. Let them know that you're not going to go away!
10) Keep all your responses, and notes of any phone calls you've made, in the same file.

> **TOP TIP**
> If you don't know who to send your letter to, write to 'The Manager' (of a shop) or 'The Director' (of a company).

YOUR LOCAL COUNCIL

If you are worried about a local problem, contact the Council Officers at the Town Hall. Your best allies when it comes to tackling local pollution are:

* the **Environmental Health Officers** who must keep the area clean and healthy, and who can prosecute polluters. Sadly, they don't always have the time or funds to solve every problem, so they need all the help they can get. You can help by reporting environmental problems.

* **Nature Conservation Officers**, who are responsible for looking after important wildlife sites.

* **Recycling Officers** who organise recycling facilities.

* **Planning Officers** who consider applications to build new buildings and other developments – they should consult local people and take account of the environmental pros and cons.

Not all Councils use exactly the same job titles – but every Council will have someone responsible for each of these areas of work.

Find out the name of the officers at your local council. You can get this information from the Town Hall. Write their details here for handy reference.

Environmental Health
Officer_____
Phone No _____

Nature Conservation
Officer_____
Phone No _____

Recycling

Officer _____

Phone No _____

Planning

Officer _____

Phone No _____

SIX WAYS TO WIN OVER YOUR COUNCIL

1) If the relevant Officer can't help, or if you want the Council to change its policy, you'll have to involve the Councillor. Councillors are responsible for particular subjects, just like Officers. If you're involved in a major campaign you'll need to get to know the Councillors too.

2) Get local people on your side. Get them to put pressure on the Council.

3) Know your stuff - the Council will take you more seriously.

4) Don't expect overnight success. Councils move slowly.

5) Don't accept 'we can't afford it' as an answer!

6) Expect to win! Friends of the Earth local groups have had great successes with their Councils. Why not you too?

USE YOUR LOCAL MP

MPs are very influential people. They can help your campaign by pulling strings with the Council or other groups in your area. They are also influential on a *national* scale, sometimes internationally too. They can write or speak directly about issues with the right Ministers.

'Lobbying' your MP is a top eco warrior activity. It means writing to him or her, and sometimes meeting up to talk about your concerns or to hand over petitions. You can meet your MP either at the House of Commons (make an appointment first) or at their surgery (that's MP speak for their local office). Your local library will have details of when and where the surgeries are.

Your MP is meant to represent all the voters in his or her constituency. However, many MPs tend to stick to their Party's views. They will usually take more notice if you represent a larger group of people, for example all the children in your school or all the residents of your street or estate. So organise a big group to go along and lobby the MP, or arrange for a lot of people to write letters on the same subject or sign a petition.

Your MP will get a better understanding of a problem if they see it with their own eyes. Taking your MP for a walk around a threatened bluebell wood, beside a polluted river, or along the route of a proposed road scheme is a good opportunity for media coverage – more about this later!

Find out who your MP is and keep his/her details here for handy reference.

Name_____

Surgery Address _____

_____

Surgery times_____

Fax number_____

Your MP's House of Commons address is:
House of Commons, London SW1A 0AA.

If you don't know who your local MP is, find out at your local library. Or phone the House of Commons Information Service on 0171 219 4272.

If your MP isn't very helpful, you can write direct to a Minister. They are shuffled from job to job regularly so ring up first to make sure you've got the right name.

GOING GLOBAL

If you don't have any joy with your local council or your MP, you can always take the matter further. Your MEP could raise the matter in the European parliament.

Your local library or the Returning Officer at the Council will tell you who your MEP is.

The European Union helps regulate our Government's environmental activities. It has forced the UK Government to clean up its act on a lot of environmental issues eg on drinking water and sewage treatment.

oh no! It's a lobbying monster!

Some European laws make the eco warrior's job easier. For example, since the *Access to Information on the Environment Directive* was passed, it should be easier to get hold of facts and figures. All public bodies must now provide environmental information to anyone who asks for it, though they may charge you for doing so.

Sometimes governments from around the world get together to talk about tackling international problems. This happened at the Earth Summit in Rio, Brazil in 1992 when governments of many different countries signed agreements to protect the world's forests and wildlife, and to tackle the threat of climate change.

They also signed 'Agenda 21', a global plan to bring about *sustainable development*. This means finding ways of reducing the amount of environmental damage we're doing to a level the planet can cope with (now and forever!) so that our children and grandchildren can still enjoy life as we do. It also means sharing the Earth's resources fairly with people in poorer countries.

Local Councils are setting up committees to tackle the enormous job of making Agenda 21 a reality locally. They need local people to help with this process so get in touch.

INTERNATIONAL COMPANIES

The HUGE companies that operate across the world are very powerful. Some of them exploit the differences between different countries' laws. Some locate their factories in the countries with lower environmental standards, where they can get away with producing filthy pollution and exploiting the local workers.

For example, the oil companies, which try so hard to appear clean and green over here, have been responsible for serious pollution problems in the 'developing' world.

WHAT YOU CAN DO

✎ The Rio Agreements set at the Earth Summit are only a framework and it was left to each country to fix the details. Write to the Prime Minister asking what Britain is doing to implement the pledges made at Rio.

✎ Ask your council what they are doing to put Agenda 21 plans into action.

✎ If you hear about environmental abuses in other parts of the world, write to your MP, and to the chairman of the company concerned to protest.

Chapter 4

ALL TOGETHER NOW!

It's much easier to get things done if you get organised. Many hands make light work, as the saying goes. Why not bump up your pester power by linking up with a pack of pals and set up a campaigning group. Together you could organise talks or school assemblies.

SETTING UP A CAMPAIGNING GROUP

The great thing about being in a group is that the work can be shared. Think about school sports where each team player has a special job to do. Well, it's just the same with a campaigning group. And you can still form a great campaigning group with just a couple of friends – by taking on two jobs each!

Fundraisers
Must be good at persuading other people to part with their money! Like double glazing salesmen. Seriously though, fundraising is a great way of attracting attention to your group.

Secretary
Takes notes at meetings in case any group members fall asleep! Ideal position for anyone with a computer who can type using more than one finger.

Treasurer
Looks after any cash your campaign brings in. Must be honest and good at maths.

The chair

The spokesperson/Press Officer
Give this job to the most attractive and confident member of the group, someone who actually enjoys performing in the school play. Don't all apply at once! They must keep the media (that's the local paper(s), radio and TV stations) informed of your group's activities.

Everyone
All members of the team must be ready to deliver leaflets, petition and write letters, help find out what the public thinks about an issue and take part in demonstrations – at the drop of a hat!

FIVE CRUCIAL CAMPAIGN TIPS

1) Plan your campaign well. Before you start campaigning write down exactly what you hope to achieve – and why.

2) If your goal is a very big one, break it down into chunks that are easier to achieve. For example, rather than aiming to make your school the greenest in the world, go for a few modest improvements, such as energy saving measures, getting recycling bins around the place or proper crockery in the canteen. That way you can celebrate sooner – before setting yourself another goal.

3) List the people or organisations whose ways you want to change.

4) Get your facts right.

5) Find out what other people think. Collect statements from people who agree with the aims of your campaign and then compile your 'results' in a 'press release' (see over the page).

If you, or one of your group, has a camcorder you can make a video to show at assemblies, youth group meetings, council meetings, and to your local MP. It  could include a range of people giving their opinions – approach your friends, a Council Officer or MP, local businesses – everyone has got something interesting to say.

Get someone famous on your side and you'll almost certainly attract interest from your local papers. They'll probably print a photo of a celebrity signing your petition, particularly if you can give them a quote from the 'star' which explains your campaign.

Keep the names and addresses of local celebrities here for handy reference

VIP Number 1

Name_____

Star rating* _____

Address_____

_____

VIP number 2

Name_____

Star rating* _____

Address_____

_____

VIP number 3

Name_____

Star rating* _____

Address_____

_____

* Decide how famous your celebs are – mark them with points (or stars!) out of three

HITTING THE HEADLINES

To win your campaign you must get the public on your side. And there's no better way of reaching people than through the media. A story in the papers or on the radio will be read or heard by thousands of people.

Here's how to use your local media to get results:

*   Your story must always have an 'angle' – that's media speak for the reason why it is particularly interesting. Local papers would be keen to write about something that is affecting local people.

*   Report the good news, instead of the bad. For example, "*A third of all locals would rather cycle or walk than go by car*" sounds more positive than saying "*Most people are car potatoes!*" Always give credit where it's due.

*   Organise a stunt – anything that would make an interesting photo or radio story. You could dress up as threatened animals, cycle in gas masks, act out a short play, or take excess packaging back to its manufacturers. There are more ideas in this book.

*   Involve your MP. Present your survey results, petition or pledges to your local MP in person –

 send local newspapers a 'press release' and invite them to photograph the occasion. If your MP supports your views, s/he may be happy to pose with you.

GETTING INTO PRINT

Writing to the letters page of your local paper is a great way to get your views heard. The letters page is one of the most widely read sections of any paper. A letter printed here can reach tens of thousands of people.

There's an art to getting into print so make sure you follow our five-point plan below:

1) Keep your letter short and simple. Make one strong point and say it in 150 words or less. The most widely read letters are one sentence long!

2) Get straight to the point.

3) A fact can be useful to make your point but don't pack in too many.

4) Make sure its either typed or written clearly and give your age.

5) Enclose a photo or drawing to illustrate your point. For example, you may be asthmatic and want to see less traffic in your area; ask a friend to snap you with your inhaler alongside a busy road.

TOP TIP
If you don't spot your letter in print, don't waste time worrying. Just write again!

HOW TO GET THE PAPERS TO COVER YOUR CAMPAIGN

Invite the local press to attend any presentation you make by sending, or faxing, a 'press release' to the News Editor.

Journalists often receive hundreds of press releases each week. So do yourself a favour by making *yours* stand out from the crowd. To help you write the perfect press release, here's one we made earlier.

The press are more likely to use your story if they have a good picture to go with it. Fax your press release to the picture desk too. By including the words 'photocall' at the top of the page, you are inviting the Picture Editor to send their own photographer along to cover the event. If you can give them a good picture opportunity they are more likely to turn up. Repeat details of the time and place here for quick reference. But take your own photos too - in case the professionals are too lazy to show up.

Keep it short (just one side of A4 paper) and to the point. Get the most important information into the first couple of attention-grabbing sentences who, what, where, when and why. If there's a lot of detail to include, put it in notes at the end.

Use Really big type!

Include a quote which sums up your campaign message. The paper can print it to save themselves the trouble of interviewing you!

TOP TIP
Always send your press release well in advance. Phone to check that it has arrived and whether anyone will be covering the story.

Get straight to the point. Head your letter with the words
PRESS RELEASE - this will ensure it lands on the right desk,
rather than being binned straightaway.

* * * PRESS RELEASE * * *

Photocall: Saturday 11th January, 11.30pm,
Town Hall

On Saturday 11th January, Byker Grove Green
Gremlins will present the Friends of the
Earth **FUMING MAD** petition to local MP Sir
Sidney Slimeball at the Town Hall.
The petition is in protest at the problem of
traffic fumes and gives suggestions of what
needs to be done to clean up air quality.

*"Nine out of ten local people want the
council to reduce the amount of traffic in
town"* explains Kylie Challenger the campaign
organiser. *"That means better, cheaper buses,
and more cycle lanes"*.

For more information call Kylie Challenger or
William Warrior on 01308 12346.

Pull out the
event, time and
the place in big
bold type

Put a contact name and phone number on the bottom in case the journalist wants to
follow the story up. And keep a copy of the press release by your phone. It will
make you sound a lot more confident if journalists phone up unexpectedly.

You must send your press release and/or photos to a named contact – if you don't it could end up in the bin! Keep the names of the News and Picture Editors of your local papers on file here for handy reference.

Name of paper_____
News Editor_____
Picture Editor _____
Fax number_____
Phone number _____

Name of paper_____
News Editor_____
Picture Editor _____
Fax number_____
Phone number _____

Radio Station _____
News Editor_____
Fax number_____
Phone number _____

And finally...

If you do make it on to the radio or telly, or into your local paper, don't forget to keep tapes, videos or cuttings. Hitting the headlines takes a lot of hard work and these show how much slog you put in. They could also be your passport to a top job in later life!

Chapter five

THE POLLUTION PROBLEM

There's no escaping pollution and the problems it causes. All over the world, air, water and land are being polluted by human activities. Let's take a look at what's happening on your doorstep, starting with the air you breathe.

AIR POLLUTION IS REAL CHOKE!

In the olden days (when your grandparents were young) the air quality in this country was a serious problem. This was mainly because factories were allowed to pump polluting fumes into the air, and also because, in those days, more people had coal fires to heat their homes. The Clean Air Act of 1956 was brought in to bust the thick smoky fogs – or smogs – which were killing people. Many towns and cities were made smoke-free zones.

Yet air pollution is once again a big problem. As well as the pollution churned out from coal and oil-burning power stations and other industry, there's a new pollution problem – and it's getting worse.

Cars and other motor vehicles are the fastest growing source of air pollution in the UK today.

Air pollution doesn't just vanish into thin air – it lingers in the atmosphere. You're probably breathing it right now. In summer when the air is hot and still, strong sunlight turns pollution into smog. In severe smogs asthma sufferers often have no choice but to stay indoors.

COUGH! SPLUTTER! GASP!

All these dangerous chemicals can be found in our air. They're mainly caused by fumes from cars and polluting power stations.

CARBON MONOXIDE *can reduce the amount of oxygen that can be carried by the blood. It can cause headaches, drowsiness and even death!*

SULPHUR DIOXIDE *can cause breathing problems and acidify rainwater. Acid rain contaminates rivers, streams and lakes, destroying wildlife. It also erodes buildings.*

NITROGEN OXIDES *cause acid rain and smogs. They also reduce our resistance to infection, irritate the lungs and aggravate asthma.*

OZONE – *safe high in the sky, but not down at ground level where it can harm our throats, lungs and immune systems and damage crops and plants.*

PM10s *are tiny particles which can pass into the lungs and aggravate breathing problems. They are thought to cause 10,000 deaths in England and Wales every year.*

Cancer-causing **BENZENE**

ASTHMATICALLY SPEAKING

Asthma has been around since long before cars were invented – the ancient Egyptians used to treat it with crocodile poo! But we know that traffic fumes can make asthma much worse. One in seven children in the UK now has asthma – in some inner-city areas one child in three suffers.

ACID RAIN

Air pollution isn't just taking our breath away – it's a threat to wildlife too. Air pollution mixes with water vapour in the atmosphere to form acid rain.

This acid rain falls into rivers, lakes and streams, killing the fish and plants that live there. Acid rain also damages trees and endangers the wildlife on land. Many lakes in Norway and Sweden, covering thousands of square kilometres, are now dead or severely damaged by acid rain. Much of this blew across the sea from the UK!

But the UK has its own problems with acid rain. British trees are showing symptoms of leaf loss which are among the worst in Europe.

THE POLLUTION POLICE

The Environment Agency has been set up to protect the environment and to check that factories, farmers, power stations and sewage works don't produce more pollution than they're allowed.

Find out where your local Environment Agency office is and keep their number here for handy reference.

Local officer's name_____

Phone number_____

OVER TO YOU!

✎ Speak out against air pollution. Write to your local paper with your views. Enclose a photo or drawing to illustrate your point.

✎ Become a dirty diesel spotter! Sooty particles from diesel engines are especially dangerous since they are small enough to pass into your lungs. Report smoky diesel lorries, buses or coaches to the Vehicle Inspectorate Enforcement Group at your local Traffic Area Office. They'll need to know the vehicle registration number, the type of vehicle, and the date, time and place you saw it. So always carry a pen and notebook.

☎ Call your Council's Environmental Health Officer and ask them to test the air for pollution. If they haven't been testing, insist that they start.

☎ Check your local air quality by phoning the Government's free Pollution Help Line on 0800 556677. If air quality keeps being poor, why not write and tell your local paper, and/or MP.

Sadly there are some lesser known forms of pollution even in your own home. Like noise pollution when dad sings in the shower! To put a stop to such practices simply photocopy this sticker and whop it on your bathroom door.

NO
SINGING
BY ORDER!

THE OZONE LAYER

Air pollution isn't just a problem at ground level. It's causing some pretty scary changes in the upper atmosphere too.

Ozone is poisonous at ground level, but the ozone layer 20-30 kilometres up in the sky is crucial to life on Earth. It protects us from the Sun's ultraviolet (UV) light. Too much UV can cause skin cancers and eye diseases, and harm plants and animals.

In 1985 scientists found a hole in the ozone layer. This hole lies above Antarctica and is getting bigger all the time. But it's not just the poles that are affected. The ozone layer is thinning over parts of Britain and Europe too. Air pollution is eating it away.

So far, about ten per cent of the Earth's ozone shield has been destroyed.

A number of chemicals which are released into the atmosphere by humans damage the ozone layer. The main problems are:

Chlorofluorocarbons (CFCs) *were found in aerosols, insulation foams, fridges, air conditioning and as metal cleaners in engineering and electronics. They are now banned in Europe.*

Hydrochlorofluorocarbons (HCFCs) *are replacing CFCs for some uses. They are safer than CFCs but do still destroy ozone. There are completely ozone-friendly alternatives.*

Methyl bromide is *a pesticide used by farmers, especially growing fruit and flowers.*

The ozone layer can only recover if these chemicals are phased out.

If all ozone-destroying substances were banned tomorrow you would be at least 60 by the time the ozone layer heals over. Every year we continue to use ozone-destroying chemicals delays its recovery by nearly another four years.

Some international companies use CFCs in other countries even though they are banned in Britain.

 Add your voice to the call to save the ozone layer. Write to the Environment Minister, asking him to persuade our own and other governments to set an early phase-out date for HCFCs and methyl bromide.

STINKING WATER

Clean water is essential for life. Amazingly, in the UK this precious resource isn't properly protected from pollution. In 1992, about a quarter of all homes in England and Wales were supplied pesticide-polluted drinking water.

Ever wondered what happens to your bath water once you've pulled the plug out? Or where your body waste goes once you've flushed the loo? It all goes to sewage treatment works to be broken down and separated into sludge and liquid 'effluent'. Often, the effluent does not get enough treatment before it is poured into rivers or the sea. This can result in pollution.

Sewage poisons wildlife. It uses up oxygen as it breaks down, leaving less for the wildlife in the water. In hot summers, sewage pollution encourages algae to grow much faster. They bloom in vast numbers and can take up all the oxygen, killing fish and other water life. Sometimes the blooms are poisonous.

Oil spills at sea kill birds and other marine life.

- One of the biggest river polluters is waste from sewage treatment. A stretch of the River Lea downstream of the Luton Sewage works consists of 90 per cent sewage effluent.

There were over 25,000 proven water pollution incidents in England and Wales in 1993.

- Sewage can be treated so it is less polluting. For example, it can be given an extra 'secondary' treatment using bacteria and other small organisms to break it down more. Secondary treatment reduces the effluent's need for oxygen, leaving more for the fish and river animals to breathe.

Enough crude oil to fill about 1,154 Olympic-sized swimming pools has been spilt at sea since 1975.

- Every day hundreds of millions of gallons of raw or virtually untreated sewage are pumped into the sea around the coast of England and Wales. Sewage contains bacteria and viruses that can give swimmers and surfers ear, eye, skin and stomach infections.

LAND POLLUTION

Pollution poured or spilled on land seeps into the ground and threatens our water supply. About a third of our tap water comes from (under)ground water. Once polluted, groundwater is almost impossible to clean up.

It's hard to keep waste on the ground...

...Eventually it will find its way into the water environment.

- Industrial waste containing toxic chemicals is often discharged into rivers from factories, directly or indirectly via the sewers. When it is poured on the ground...

   ...these chemicals can seep down to pollute underground water supplies.

- farm chemicals such as nitrates (found in fertilizers) and pesticides sprayed on crops...

   ...get washed by the rain into our rivers, streams and seas. Some pesticides build up in plants and harm the animals that feed on them.

- farm waste such as pig slurry...

   ...can cause disastrous pollution if it leaks out of stores into nearby rivers.

- rubbish dumps...

   ...when rubbish rots down, harmful liquids can leak out and pollute rivers and groundwater.

THE POLLUTION SOLUTION

Five things the Government must do to clean up the country

1) Make public transport more reliable, cheaper and comfortable so more people actually prefer to use it. And encourage rail use, particularly for long distance freight. They should also reduce our need to travel so much... for example, by banning new out-of-town shopping centres.

2) Insist that coal-fired power stations filter their fumes to remove most of the sulphur dioxide. This is a very effective way of reducing acid rain.

3) Promote renewable energy sources (see chapter 8)

4) Treat sewage effluent enough so that is is not harmful to swimmers and surfers.

5) Encourage industry to develop cleaner processes which use less resources and produce less pollution.

Five ways you can help

1) Don't drop litter yourself and ask other children not to.

2) Cut down your energy consumption! (see chapter 8)

3) Never use more water than you need. Our demand for water is so great these days that water companies are draining rivers to cope. The less water rivers contain, the more concentrated any pollution becomes.

4) Recycle your rubbish to reduce waste – there's more about this in the next chapter.

5) Encourage your folks to become green shoppers! Give aerosols the big E! Although they don't contain CFCs any more, they do contain other polluting chemicals and can't be recycled. Buy recycled goods and organic food. There's more about this on page 119.

RIVER POLLUTION:
DON'T SWALLOW IT!

☎Report all signs of river pollution to the pollution police. Phone the Environment Agency Hotline on 0800 807060 if you spot scum, dead fish and water which smells or has changed colour. Calls are free.

Your local Environmental Agency Officers need your help in spotting the first signs of pollution. They can act quickly to track down the polluters and make them pay. They can also give you information about local companies and farmers who are 'legally' dirtying rivers and streams in your area and others who are producing more pollution than they should. Armed with the facts you can...

✎ Write to the Prime Minister. Ask for stronger laws preventing industry and farms from dumping dangerous toxins in rivers. And ask for tougher punishments for those that break the law.

✎ Make polluters sit up and take notice of the pollution problem in your area. Send them a bottle of stinky river water, with one of the special labels printed here. Fill an old bottle with local river water, then cut out* and stick on a *Thirst-stencher* label.

WARNING!
Never, <u>ever</u> go near rivers without a grown up accompanying you. Playing near rivers is very dangerous! And wash your hands after filling the bottle!

TOP TIP
Delivering your bottle by hand will save you postage and packing costs! As well as making a nice photo opportunity for the local press.

Enclose a letter with your bottle of water. Explain that you are seriously concerned about water pollution and the effects it is having on the environment. Ask them to stop it – now!

Well, I was feeling thirsty but now I'm not so sure!

*Thirst-stencher!
THE NEW RIVER WATER DRINK

BOTTLED AT SOURCE

_____

(write the name of the river where you took this sample from in here)

Ingredients:
Farm waste including pigs poo!
Poisonous metals
Pesticides
Chemical Cocktail
Nitrates from fertilisers
Sewage

DO **NOT** DRINK

*Photocopy this label if you don't want to cut up your book

We interrupt this book to bring you a bit of
light relief... so take a break and find out

HOW GREEN

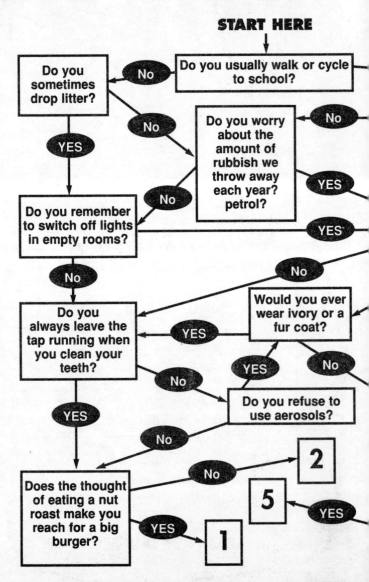

START HERE

Do you usually walk or cycle to school?

Do you sometimes drop litter?

Do you worry about the amount of rubbish we throw away each year? petrol?

Do you remember to switch off lights in empty rooms?

Do you always leave the tap running when you clean your teeth?

Would you ever wear ivory or a fur coat?

Do you refuse to use aerosols?

Does the thought of eating a nut roast make you reach for a big burger?

No · No · No · YES · YES · No · No · No · YES · YES · YES · No · YES · No · No · YES · 1 · 2 · 5

Test your green rating with our quick quiz

ARE YOU?

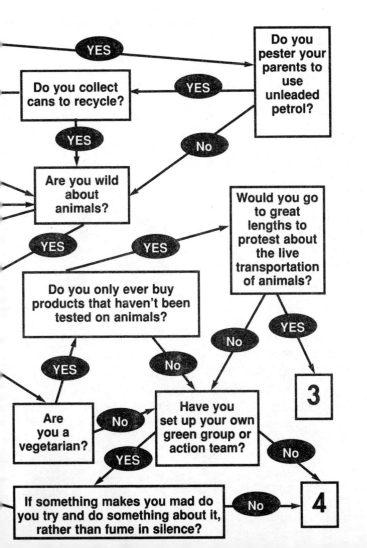

Do you pester your parents to use unleaded petrol?

Do you collect cans to recycle?

YES

YES

YES

Are you wild about animals?

No

Would you go to great lengths to protest about the live transportation of animals?

YES

YES

Do you only ever buy products that haven't been tested on animals?

No

No

YES

3

Are you a vegetarian?

No

Have you set up your own green group or action team?

No

YES

If something makes you mad do you try and do something about it, rather than fume in silence?

No

4

Well, how well did you do?

1 Gadzooks! Your green rating is so low it's almost off the scale. But at least you're reading this book. By the time you've finished it, you're going to know a lot more about the planet's problems and what you can do about them. So don't waste any more time... turn to chapter six now!

2 Hmm! You're keen on becoming green though you're not exactly putting yourself out to help the planet. The fact that you're reading this book is a start. But come on, you can try a bit harder...

3 You know that we've all got to do our bit to help protect the planet. But your big passion is for animals. In fact, you're wild about them, and you'd do a lot to stop them suffering. You'd rather go naked than wear a fur coat and you think ivory looks better on elephants!

4 You're a real keen greenie. You're worried about using up the Earth's natural resources so you try to recycle waste and save energy whenever you can. You know the power of pestering and you're chomping at the bit to help change the ways of the world and clean up the planet. Go for it!

5 You're so green it would be hard to spot you in a bowl full of gooseberries! You do everything you can to save the Earth. You're certainly not afraid of causing a stink! You've even set up a green group to make your local environment a cleaner, greener place to live. Hooray!

Chapter six

ONCE IS NOT ENOUGH!

Every year in the UK we throw away 20 million tonnes of rubbish from our homes. That's nearly one tonne for each household.

Our wasteful ways mean double pressure on the environment: coping with the waste, and supplying ever more raw materials, which will become the waste of tomorrow.

Most of our household rubbish ends up on landfill tips, where it rots down, generating methane gas and poisonous liquids. The rest is burned, creating polluting smoke, and ash.

Everything we use has to come from somewhere. Wildlife habitats are damaged and pollution caused when resources are mined, harvested and refined to make everyday products like newspapers and cans.

It's time we dumped the 'throwaway society' in the dustbin of history. This chapter will show you some of the ways in which you can help take the pressure off the planet.

Reducing rubbish makes better use of the Earth's precious resources. There's no point in chucking things out if they can be repaired or reused.

If waste can't be reused or repaired then recycling is the answer. **Recycling** means using the same materials again to make new products. Many materials can be recycled over and over and over again.

Lots of things in this list can be recycled. But do you know which? Put a tick by any items you think can be used again:

☐ Glass Bottles

☐ Aluminium cans

☐ Steel cans

☐ Plastic wrapping

☐ Leftover food

☐ Embarrasingly un-hip Turtles T-Shirt

☐ Detention note from teacher

☐ Dad's corny jokes

How many did you tick? You may be surprized to know that all of the items on this list can be recycled. Just take a look...

GLASS BOTTLES

Bottles can be reused, many times over, saving energy. The best known example is the doorstep pinta, milk bottles are refilled up to a hundred times.

Old smashed bottles and jars can be melted down to make new glass. This saves energy and raw materials. Quarrying sand and limestone for new glass is also damaging for the environment.

TOP TIP: Always buy milk in glass bottles rather than in paper cartons – and sent them back to be refilled.

ALUMINIUM AND STEEL CANS

All food and drink cans can be melted down and made into cans again, with enormous energy savings compared with making new cans. Sadly, of the 42 million cans used in the UK every day, only 22% are recycled.

CAN BAN! In Denmark it is illegal to sell drinks in cans! The Danish Government passed this law so that refillable bottles are used as much as possible.

PLASTIC

Plastic can be recycled, but there are very few facilities to collect it and less than one per cent of plastic from households is recycled in the UK. Ask your local authority to set up plastic recycling points.

LEFT OVERS

All organic matter such as fruit and vegetable peelings, stale food, lawn clippings and leaves, and even your hamster's poo can be composted to nourish your flower beds or pot plants!

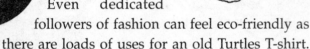

TOP TIP
Don't forget you can feed your pets on kitchen scraps.

EMBARRASINGLY OLD-FASHIONED TURTLES T-SHIRT

Even dedicated followers of fashion can feel eco-friendly as there are loads of uses for an old Turtles T-shirt. For a start, someone else might want to wear it.

Failing that, it could be pulled apart and respun – who knows, it might even morph itself into a Power Rangers T-shirt. Seriously though, old clothes can be used to make new clothes, furniture stuffing, blankets and roofing felt.

DETENTION NOTE FROM TEACHER

Don't bin paper – it can be recycled to make toilet rolls, tissues, or more notepaper for teachers and other lifeforms.

DAD'S CORNY JOKES

There's no such thing as a new joke, just an updated one. Even a joke you've only just heard is likely to have been around since the Jurassic era. But don't let that wipe the smile off your face. There will always be someone who hasn't heard it yet!

RECYCLING AT HOME

Find out from the Council where your local recycling facilities are. Keep the details for handy reference.

The nearest bottle bank to my home is

_____

_____

My nearest paper recycling point is

_____

_____

TOP TIP
Set up recycling schemes at school. Invite the Council Recycling Officer in for a meeting to discuss the possibilities.

My nearest can recycling point is

_____

_____

My nearest plastics recycling point is

_____

_____

List of local shops who will use old carrier bags

_____

_____

_____

Some councils collect recyclables from people's houses. For example Leeds City Council gives people two bins. One is for packaging, textiles and newspapers; the other one has separate compartments for organic waste and non-recyclables. 45% of these people's rubbish is being recycled.

Charity shop I can send my old toys and books to

_____

_____

_____

_____

_____

CAMPAIGNING IDEAS

✎ If your recycling banks are always full, ask the Council to provide more. Work out how many collection points there are per person for different materials in your area. First find out the number of people living in your borough or district (ask at your local council or library). Then simply divide this number by the number of recycling points of each type. The local press may be interested in your findings.

🚩 When you next visit a fast food restaurant, ask for a proper plate and knife and fork! Few outlets actually recycle the mountain of expanded polystrene, paper cartoons and cups and plastic cutlery they dole out each day.

🚩 Compost your kitchen waste. If you haven't got a garden you can use an indoor 'worm-bin'. You need a plastic dustbin and some special compost worms (also called Brandling or manure worms) – you can buy these from anglers' shops. Feed the worms on food scraps and they will turn them into compost for your pot plants.

WARNING
FAILING TO ASK A PARENT'S PERMISSION BEFORE MAKING A WORMERY COULD SERIOUSLY AFFECT YOUR POCKET MONEY

RUBBISH SURVEY

Carry out a survey to discover how many people recycle their rubbish and, if not, whether they would if the facilities were available. Photocopy the form below and hand it out to people in your class, school or street.

Which of these do you recycle? (please tick)

☐ Glass

☐ Paper

☐ Metal

☐ Old clothes or goods
(giving to a charity shop or jumble sale is a form of recycling)

☐ Compostable material

☐ Plastic

Which of these would you recycle if the facilities were close by?

☐ Glass

☐ Paper

☐ Metal

☐ Old clothes or goods

☐ Compostable material

☐ Plastic

✎ You can use the results of this survey to campaign for improved recycling facilities in your area. Find out whether your Council is anywhere near meeting the Government's 25 per cent recycling target (see the next page). If not, write and ask them why. Your local paper may be interested in the story.

WHAT A DUMP!

Only five per cent of household waste is currently being recycled.

The Government aims to recycle 25% by the year 2000 – it had better get a move on! Even this isn't really an ambitious target. The Government reckons that 70 per cent could be recycled.

Rubbish from homes is not the only problem. Every year a staggering 460 million tonnes of waste are thrown away from shops, offices, factories, farms, building sites, mines and quarries.

Hundreds of landfill rubbish dumps pose a serious risk of polluting water or air. And landfill is no longer the easy option it once was, as space for new dumps is running out near to cities. The new stricter environmental controls make landfilling more expensive too. This makes incineration a favoured alternative.

Incineration doesn't 'dispose' of waste. It just reduces its volume by about two thirds, leaving toxic ash which is usually landfilled. Smoke and gases given off when waste is burned in incinerators can contain dioxins, which are harmful to health even at very low levels.

Recycling helps stop the rot!

WRAP ATTACK

About one third of the rubbish in the average dustbin is packaging.

Manufacturers like packaging. It can make their products seem bigger or better than they really are. They will only reduce their packaging if customers demand simpler wrapping.

If you look closely, you'll be surprised at how much packaging is a waste of space. Unwrap a week's shopping in one go and take a look.

How many layers of packaging are there?
How much is really needed?
Can it be refilled?
Is it made of recycled materials?
Can you recycle it?

Work out who are the worst offenders and send them a wrap attack award. Photocopy the one opposite or design one of your own if you don't want to cut up this book.

OUT OF EVERY £75 SPENT ON GROCERIES, £10 IS FOR THE PACKAGING.

WRAP ATTACK AWARD

CONGRATULATIONS!

PLEASE ACCEPT THIS
WRAP ATTACK
AWARD WITH MY COMPLIMENTS

_____

THE ABOVE NAMED PRODUCT IS
OVERPACKAGED AND SO CAUSES
UNNECESSARY WASTE.

PLEASE PACK IT IN!
I WILL NOT BE BUYING THIS
PRODUCT AGAIN UNTIL YOU
REDUCE ITS PACKAGING

Signed _____ date _____
Name and address _____
_____

EASTER EGG PACKAGING – WHAT A YOLK!

Easter comes but once a year, and when it does it brings... a load of rubbish.

We all enjoy eating Easter eggs but most of us are shocked at the amount of fancy packaging they come in. Show your disapproval next Easter by following these five steps:

1) Carefully unwrap your Easter egg and remove the egg.

2) Weigh the egg.

3) Weigh the packaging.

4) Work out what to do with all that card, plastic and tin foil.

5) Send it back to the chocolate manufacturers, so that they can see with their own eyes how wasteful their packaging is.

Fill in and cut out the coupon opposite. Then piece the packaging back together and stick the coupon where the egg used to be. Pop it in the plastic shell if it has one. Now post the entire carton back to the chocolate manufacturers' head office. The address should be on the packaging.

Dear

_____

I enjoyed scoffing my delicious

_____

Easter egg, but I'm angry about the amount of cardboard and plastic it came wrapped in.

Rather than waste all that packaging – especially that plastic bit in the middle, which will probably still be around when I'm buying eggs for my children – I am returning it to you in the hope that you will do the decent thing and recycle it.

And I won't be buying another Easter egg from you next year unless you rethink and reduce your packaging.

Yours sincerely

_____ *aged* _____

And finally...

Don't be a wicked waster! Remember the 3 R's of recycling:

Refuse to be given unnecessary packaging.

Reuse as much as you can. Items such as envelopes and plastic bags can all be reused. Take unwanted clothes and toys to a charity shop. Buy **refillable** bottles whenever you can and make sure you **return** them. **Repair** things rather than throw them away.

Recycle paper, cans and bottles. Get recycling systems sorted at school. Encourage your family to recycle rubbish wherever possible. Cut out this label and stick it onto the lid of your kitchen swing bin.

STOP!
DO NOT ATTEMPT TO THROW THIS
AWAY IF IT CAN BE RECYCLED!

Chapter Seven

OUR DISAPPEARING WORLD

Millions of years ago much of the Earth was covered in lush forest. Only 500 years ago most of the tropical rainforests were still undisturbed. But today these forests are disappearing and deserts are taking their place.

During your lifetime, people all over the world have been campaigning to save the rainforests. And yet an area the size of England and Wales is **still** lost each year. Wildlife is being wiped out, people are losing their homes and livelihoods, and it's even affecting the world's climate.

Tropical rainforests must be protected because they:

- **are home to 200 million tribal people.**

- **support ecosystems that include millions of different plants and animals.**

- **help keep the Earth's climate constant. Deforested areas become hotter and dryer. Forests soak up carbon dioxide (a greenhouse gas) and breathe out oxygen, which we need to live.**

It's hypocritical for us in the chilly North to tell foreign governments to protect their forests while we keep on destroying our own woods and countryside.

Between a third and a half of Britain's ancient woodlands have been lost in the last fifty years. Once, England had so many trees that a squirrel could have hopped from Sherwood Forest in Nottingham to Lands End in Cornwall without touching the ground.

The great 'temperate' forests in Canada and the USA are being given the chop too. Huge areas of forest, home to giant 1,000-year-old trees, elk, bears and wolves, have been destroyed by timber and paper companies. And in Scandinavia, logging is the single largest threat to wildlife. Many hundreds of species face extinction.

So why are we using all this wood?

A lot of our woodland is cleared to make room for roads, quarries and new shopping and housing developments.

Many of the trees cut down in North America and Scandinavia go to feed the world's demands for timber and paper. We use wood from the tropical rainforests to make furniture, doors, windows and fittings for shops and pubs.

The UK is one of the world's largest timber consumers. Every year we get through about 25 million cubic metres of timber. As much again goes to produce our paper.

WHAT YOU CAN DO

If enough people protest, governments will force industry to use wood more sustainably. You can start the ball rolling by organising a petition and sending it to local timber yards and your MP. There are lots of other ways you can protect the world's trees too.

For a start you can curb your consumption of paper. Recycle any paper you use. Get your school to make notebooks from paper that's printed on one side only.

Alert your family to the horrors of buying tropical hardwoods such as mahogany. Most of the mahogany sold over here comes from Brazil's Amazon rainforest. Much of it is logged illegally in Indian reserves. The loggers who plunder the forests bring disease and destruction with them.

Go on the look out for 'stolen' mahogany around your home. You may find this reddish-coloured wood where you'd least expect it – for example, it's often used for loo seats. Then copy this sticker and plaster it on any mahogany products you find aound the home! This will remind your parents not to buy tropical timber.

```
┌─────────────────────────────────┐
│     STOLEN PROPERTY!             │
│  This product may be made from   │
│ mahogany stolen from the disappearing │
│  Brazilian rainforest. Save the planet │
│      – don't buy mahogany!       │
└─────────────────────────────────┘
```

It's not just woods that are fast disappearing in Britain. Every year, more and more of our meadows, peat-bogs and hedgerows are torn apart by road-building, quarrying, mining, housing developments, peat-cutting and farming.

- Since the 1940s, we've lost or harmed at least half of our fens and wetlands and nearly all of our flower-rich meadows. A traditional hay meadow had over 100 different kinds of wild flowers and was home to many insects, especially butterflies, and small mammals such as field mice.

- Peat bogs play a significant role in helping control the global climate. They soak up carbon dioxide and can store it for thousands of years. They are also important wildlife sanctuaries. Yet some of Britain's oldest peat bogs are under threat. Companies dig peat up to sell to gardeners.

- **Modern farming methods can be bad for wildlife. Chemical pesticides and fertilizers, and farm wastes such as slurry, are a big pollution problem. Farmers have removed miles of hedges to make their fields bigger.**

- **More than 200 of our best wild places, known as Sites of Special Scientific Interest (SSSIs) are damaged or destroyed every year.**

Gone but not forgotten – five extinct British species

1) Greater Mouse-Eared Bat
2) Vipers Bugloss Moth
3) Red-Backed Shrike
4) Meadow Wood Ant
5) Orange-Spotted Emerald Dragonfly

...and five that soon could be

1) Corncrake
2) Harbour Porpoise
3) Sturgeon
4) Southern Damselfly
5) Shore Dock

Three animals I'd like to see protected:

_____

_____

_____

IT'S A FACT:
OUR DISAPPEARING COUNTRYSIDE:

In the UK...

- At least 10,000 hectares of land are swallowed up by out-of-town developments each year. That's 13,888 football pitches worth of land! It's time we blew the final whistle on them!

- An area twice the size of Birmingham is devoted to vehicle parking.

- There are over 360,000 kilometres of road. Mountains of gravel, sand and other materials were needed to build them, leaving gaping holes around the countryside.

Save our countryside before its too late!

OVER TO YOU

Learn about local wildlife sites and make sure they're safe. If you hear about plans to build on one, campaign to save it. Involve the media and your MP. Contact the local Friends of the Earth group

Become a super sleuth! Scan your local paper for planning applications for any new developments (supermarkets, warehouses etc) that will threaten land near you. All applications have to be publicised via local papers, often using sneakily small print!

WILD ABOUT ANIMALS? THEN GET MAD!

We've encroached on so much of the world's wildest places that many magnificent creatures may become extinct.

About 5,000 animal species are endangered. This means their numbers are decreasing and that they may die out forever. Here's five of the most endangered animals on the planet:

Mediterranean Monk Seal
There are only about 500 of these shy seals left in the Mediterranean waters around Greece.

Golden Lion Tamarin
This maned monkey was actually thought to be extinct until a small colony of them was found in the Brazilian rainforest.

Yangtze River Dolphins
The rarest dolphin on Earth – only about 300 remain.

Spix's Macaw
One of the world's rarest birds – there's only one left in the wild.

Chinese Tiger
These beautiful creatures have been hunted to death. There are only about 50 alive today.

It's important not only to protect individual species but the whole network of living things. Friends of the Earth is very concerned with **biodiversity** – a technical term which means the variety of life.

At the 1992 Rio Earth Summit, over 150 world leaders signed up to a Convention to conserve biodiversity worldwide. Sadly, few solid plans have been made to put this into practice and habitats and species continue to decline. But it's not all doom and gloom: there's lots you can do to protect the biodiversity of British wildlife.

A well-cared-for garden is a fine example of biodiversity. It can support a huge variety of wildlife, providing a refuge for 30 different bird species, a dozen butterflies, half a dozen small mammals, 20 orders of insects, 200 different plants and literally thousands of different micro-organisms.

OVER TO YOU

☐ Create a wildlife garden, at home or at school. Grow plants that attract wildlife. If you've got space, plant a tree (choose a native species such as oak or hawthorn).

☐ Make a pond to provide a home for aquatic life and somewhere for other animals to drink – we need to replace some of those lost wetlands.

☐ If cats enter your garden they will be a serious hazard to your birds and frogs, so provide a safe bird table in an area where cats can't pounce.

☐ Be a green gardener. Don't use artificial chemicals. And don't use peat. Make your own compost to boost the soil's growing power.

Chapter Eight

TAKING THE HEAT OFF THE PLANET

Few things affect the environment as much as our use of energy. Energy is used in almost everything we do, from cooking food and lighting our homes to smelting iron ore and powering car engines.

Like many industrialised countries, the UK uses a lot of energy. In fact, we are the world's seventh biggest energy user. The average person in the UK uses more than ten times more energy than the average person in India.

All this energy we're using, and wasting, is damaging the planet.

Fossil Fuels

In the UK, 91% of our energy comes from 'fossil fuels': coal, oil and gas. These were formed over millions of years from the fossilised remains of dead animals and plants. Once burned, they can never be replaced. So unless we cut back on energy waste, there won't be any fossil fuels left for your grandchildren

Fossil fuels are either burned in power stations to make electricity, or we burn them ourselves – gas in our homes, petrol in our cars.

Unfortunately, burning fossil fuels releases carbon into the atmosphere, which causes global warming. Power stations also produce other pollution, which cause acid rain and affect people's health.

Every year, each man, woman and child in the UK uses the equivalent of more than 18,411 litres of oil – that's about 51 bath tubs full!

If all the barrels of oil produced in a day in the world were laid end to end, the line would stretch twice around the equator.

Nuclear energy

Only six per cent of our electricity is produced by nuclear power. Nuclear power doesn't directly produce carbon dioxide or acid rain gases. But it does produce highly dangerous radioactive waste. This gives off radiation which is so deadly it must be kept out of harm's way for thousands of years. Yet there's no way of doing this safely.

There's a higher than normal incidence of leukaemia in children in the area around Sellafield, a big nuclear fuel plant in Cumbria, England.

The threat of an accident at a nuclear plant is almost too frightening to think about. In 1986, a power station at Chernobyl in the Ukraine, exploded killing 32 people, injuring hundreds of others and affecting sheep up to 2,000 miles away in North Wales! Thousands of people are still suffering the after effects of that disaster. Yet with over 350 nuclear reactors operating in the world, chances are that there will be another major accident before the end of the century. Say no to nuclear power!

The good news is that no more nuclear power stations are going to be built in Britain – thanks to years of campaigning by Friends of the Earth and others.

RENEWABLE ENERGY

And again on the bright side, there are alternatives to fossil fuels which are cleaner, safer and more importantly, won't run out! 'Renewable' energy captures the inexhaustible energy of the wind, water, wave and sun. Wind energy alone could supply at least 20 per cent of the UK's electricity.

But we'd better get a move on. For our greedy guzzling of fossil fuels is causing global warming – it's making the planet too hot for our own good!

THE GREENHOUSE EFFECT AND GLOBAL WARMING

The most serious effect of us using all this energy is the rising amount of carbon dioxide being pumped into the atmosphere. Levels are higher today than at any other time in history.

Before this century there was just about the right amount of 'greenhouse gases' (such as carbon dioxide, methane, nitrous oxide and CFCs) in the atmosphere to keep the Earth at just about the right temperature. Greenhouse gases make an insulating layer around the Earth, a bit like the glass in a greenhouse, to trap in the heat of the Sun's rays. This is called the Greenhouse Effect and in itself, it's very valuable. Without it the Earth would be an incredible 32°C colder than it is now and life as we know it could not exist.

But over the last 100 years, scientists have noticed a phenomenon they call 'global warming'. They think the planet is getting warmer because industrialised countries, like Britain with its many factories and millions of cars, are pumping more 'greenhouse gases' into the atmosphere than ever before. It is almost as though another layer of double glazing has been added around the Earth. The coolest parts of the planet – the polar ice caps have started to melt!

1995 was one of the hottest years on record. On the first of August 1995 a temperature of 95.3°F was recorded in Cambridge – the highest summer temperature since August 1990 when it reached a scorching 98.7°F, the official highest temperature ever recorded in the UK!

By 2030 the level of carbon dioxide in the atmosphere may be twice that of the last century. This means the Earth will keep on getting hotter, the ice caps will keep melting and that as a result sea levels will be about 20 centimetres higher than they are today. Low-lying parts of North Wales, East Anglia and the Thames estuary may be drowned. There will be more drought and famine and many plants and animals will become extinct. The last time the Earth's climate changed like this, the largest living creatures, the dinosaurs, died out.

It's time for action before we're all sunk!

The Earth can only heal itself if we:

- stop burning so much fossil fuel and use cleaner safer kinds of power – such as wind, wave or sun power – instead, which store carbon dioxide safely.

- use cars less. Cars produce carbon dioxide and other greenhouse gases.

- Curb our cow consumption! Fast food has become such big business that there's now an amazing 1,280,000,000 cattle in the world. An estimated 15% of all the methane gas in the atmosphere is farted out by cows and other cud-chewing animals.

- Ban all CFCs and related greenhouse gases. Their use is now banned in aerosols but they're still used in fridges, and air conditioning systems. 100 million American cars are cooled by air-conditioning systems built to use CFCs! Industry must make safe alternatives to them – now!

WAR ON WASTE...

The way we generate and use electricity in the UK is a good example of this problem.

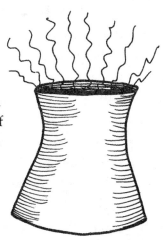

Nearly every power station in Britain wastes more than half of the energy in coal, oil and uranium when it converts it into electricity. The waste comes out as steam, allowed to escape into the atmosphere via huge cooling towers. By changing the design of power stations, this energy could be put to work instead. For example, Combined Heat and Power (or CHP) stations trap 'waste' heat, which can be used to heat homes and factories nearby. CHP schemes are common in European cities but not in the UK.

✎ *Write to the Prime Minister asking the Government to invest more in renewable sources of energy. According to their own figures, up to half of our energy could be generated from wind turbines sited at sea. Tell the PM that you are concerned about the wasted energy that flows from Britain's power stations. Ask him why the Government does not make use of this energy to heat homes and offices.*

✎ *Highly dangerous nuclear waste is moved around the country by train. Write to your council and ask them whether nuclear fuel actually passes through your area. If it does you can ask your council to put a ban on this!*

BE A SUPER SAVER!

There are more ways to save energy than by going to bed an hour earlier and getting up an hour later. Even though you might miss double maths this way. Here's seven things you can do to take the heat off the planet:

1) Turn off the TV and go read a book! About two power stations are needed just to operate Britain's 38.3 million household television sets. And the 17 million Coronation Street audience needs its very own power station.

2) Turn off lights in empty rooms and all electrical appliances if they're not in use.

3) If you feel chilly put on a jumper instead of turning up the central heating!

4) If it's hot at school, ask for the heating to be turned down rather than opening windows.

5) Walk or cycle whenever it is safe to do so (see chapter nine).

6) Don't waste your hot bath water. Someone else could use it after you've finished.

7) Only fill the kettle with as much water as you need.

Friends of the Earth believes that everybody could easily cut their energy consumption by 30 per cent without noticing the difference. Only your parents can help you meet this target as saving large amounts of energy requires a commitment to better insulating your home, going without gas guzzling cars more and replacing poorly designed appliances with energy-efficient ones.

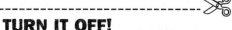

TURN IT OFF!
Only real energy wasters leave the TV on standby. So don't be a couch potato – get up and switch it off properly.

Encourage everyone in your family to save energy by switching the TV set off at the mains when it is not being watched. A colour TV switched off by the remote control only can still use a quarter of that used when it's on. In 1989 Friends of the Earth calculated that TVs on standby were using more than £12 million of electricity a year – that's enough to provide all the electric power to a town the size of Burnley or Basingstoke. So cut out this label and stick it onto your TV remote control today!

FAMILY MATTERS

It's time to sit your parents down and have a serious talk with them about saving energy.

Ask them to think seriously about taking energy-saving steps in the home. Remind them that although some of these will cost money, the good news is that they will actually save more on cheaper fuel bills, year after year! For example, fitting a jacket to your water heating cylinder costs about £8 but saves about £13.50 each year. Some steps won't cost parents a penny but will still save them pounds. For example, turning the thermostat down by one degree, or using an hour less heating a day, saves about £32 a year.

As making your home more energy efficient takes effort parents may need an incentive to make changes. Use the pledge opposite to strike a bargain with mum/dad. If you promise to reward their troubles they can hardly refuse, can they!

WARNING!

When your family needs a new fridge make sure you choose one that contains reduced levels of CFCs. Don't dump your old fridge. Call your council and/or the fridge manufacturer and ask them to remove the old CFCs from it. These can be recycled.

To whom it concerns

I promise to

☐ insulate or improve the insulation in the loft

☐ turn down the thermostat by a few degrees

☐ draftproof the doors and windows

☐ lag the hot water tank

☐ turn off radiators in empty rooms

☐ fit aluminium foil behind radiators to reflect heat back into the room and so bump up their heating power

☐ when necessary replace any appliances (fridges, freezers, cookers, TVs etc) with energy-efficient ones

☐ buy energy-efficient, compact fluorescent light bulbs.

Signed _____

(Mum/Dad/Head of household)

...and, in return, I promise to

☐ stop nattering when the news is on

☐ keep my bedroom tidy for at least a term

☐ clean my teeth without being told to

☐ hand in a whole week's homework on time

☐ put my dirty clothes in the laundry basket instead of leaving them scattered around the house

☐ give up sweets for a week

☐ lend a hand with the washing up

☐ do an hour's gardening each weekend

(NB You must tick one box for every box ticked on your mum/dad's list)

It's a deal!

Signed _____

(You fill in this bit)

OVER TO YOU!

✎ Write to your MP and ask him/her to introduce a new law encouraging owners to insulate buildings properly, and making it cheaper for people to buy energy-efficient houses.

✎ Write to local businesses asking what they are doing to conserve energy. Keep an eye out for shops who leave their doors open all day. Think of all the heat that's pouring out onto the street. Write and remind them how wasteful this is and ask them to become more energy efficient.

✎ Write to your local council and ask them to replace all the street lamp bulbs in your area with energy-efficient, compact fluorescent ones. These give out as much light as an ordinary bulb but use a lot less energy. Some use 80 per cent less energy than ordinary ones!

⌐ Work out what and when your family uses the most energy at home. Check your electricity and gas meters every three hours for one day. You'll notice that the meters move faster when you're using more energy. Work out what activities (cooking, washing etc) 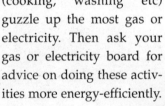 guzzle up the most gas or electricity. Then ask your gas or electricity board for advice on doing these activities more energy-efficiently.

Chapter Nine

CARS ARE A REAL CHOKE!

It's no joke. The air around us is being polluted by invisible gases which can damage our health. And although these come from many sources, motor vehicles are the fastest growing source of air pollution in the UK today. The cocktail of chemicals pumped out by motor vehicles poses a serious threat to our health. These chemicals can:

- **irritate the lungs**
- **make asthma and breathing difficulties much worse**
- **cause cancer**

and even kill us!

But cars are more than a choke! At present almost 4,000 people are killed and 300,000 injured on our roads every year. And cars hurt wildlife too. An estimated 47,000 badgers are killed each year by cars – one from every family of badgers in the country. And cars cause acid rain, which is damaging forests, rivers and streams and the wildlife that lives in them.

There are more cars on the UK's roads than ever before – over 20 million in total. 1.7 million new cars hit the streets in 1993 alone.

The Government keeps building more roads to cope with increasing traffic. But building new roads doesn't make sense. It doesn't prevent traffic jams because it simply encourages even more cars onto the roads. The Government predicts that another 10 million cars will be using our roads by 2025...

CARS COST THE EARTH

Road building is destroying the British countryside. Over the last thirty years countless important wildlife havens have been tarmacked over. As this book is being written, the Department of Transport is bull-dozing through precious countryside to build the Newbury Bypass. The nine miles the new road will cover is home for all sorts of wildlife, including adders, dormice, kingfishers and rare bats. Yet it won't solve Newbury's traffic problems.

Since 1993 all new cars have had to be fitted with catalytic converters which can cut some of the most harmful gases in car fumes by more than 75%. But this is not enough to stop pollution reaching dangerous levels, especially as car numbers keep growing.

3 good reasons to curb the car

1) Cars use lots of fuel. A full car uses around seven times more energy per person than a full double-decker bus.

2) Fewer cars on the roads means fewer road accidents.

3) Walking, even short distances is a great form of exercise. The British Heart Foundation recommends a brisk 20 minute stroll every day to keep you fit and healthy.

...and 3 things the Government must do to help

1) Make public transport more reliable, cheaper and comfortable so more people actually prefer to use it. Buses, for example, often get held up in traffic jams. Priority bus lanes would whizz them on their way.

2) Encourage rail use, particularly for long distance travel and freight. Railways are cheaper to build and maintain than roads. Big lorries are a liability: they are up to eight times more likely than cars to be involved in fatal accidents. And one big lorry causes as much road damage as 100,000 cars!

3) Make cycling safer by setting up cycle lanes in every town and city. Cycling is much safer in countries, such as Sweden, Holland and Germany, where there are good cycling facilities.

> *There are lots of ways you can help curb the car, clean up our air and save our countryside too. Here's two for starters...*
>
> *Write to your local Council and ask them to reduce motor traffic in your area.*
>
> *Tell your MP that you are fed up of being a car potato. Ask him or her to try to persuade the Minister for Transport to stop building new roads and encourage public transport and cycling instead. Use the toints above as the basis of your argument.*

CURBING THE CAR

Cars and motor vehicles are a very useful and valuable part of modern life. Ambulances save lives by speeding the sick or injured to hospital. Buses take us to shop in towns and cities. And cars carry us to work or to see friends who live miles away. But sadly many of us have become 'car potatoes'. We use the car for short journeys which could easily be walked or cycled.

If more people walked, cycled or travelled by bus or train there would be millions fewer cars polluting our air each day. and that would mean a long term improvement in air quality.

THE MOMENT OF TRUTH!

Are you a car potato? Find out by recording your family's car use over one whole week. Fill in this chart – as honestly as possible. Remember to include every car in your household, if you have more than one car. Keep this page with a pen by the front door so that you see it on returning from each journey. And don't forget to quiz your parents and other members of your family each evening about any journeys they may have made while you were out or at school.

	Day 1	Day 2	Day 3	Day 4	Day 5	Day 6	Day 7	Total
Number of car journeys made in your household								
Number of car journeys under three miles								
Number of journeys that could have been made in an alternative way (ie. by bus, train, bike or walking).								

Finished? Right, gather your family around and show them the results.

* What is the total car journeys made over the week?

☐ 0-10   ☐ 11-20   ☐ 20 or more

* How many car journeys were made under three miles?

☐ 0-5   ☐ 6-10   ☐ 11 or more

* How many car journeys could have been made in an alternative way?

☐ 0-5   ☐ 6-10   ☐ 11 or more

If you've ticked any boxes apart from the ones on the left-hand side of this page, you and your family are in danger of becoming car potatoes. It's time to think about curbing your car use. We'll tell you how – over the page.

Friends of the Earth recommends that we all leave our cars at home *at least two days a week* – and go by bike or bus, train or tram, or our own two feet instead.

- **Over three quarters of all journeys are less than five miles in length – ideal for walking or cycling.**

- **Walking and cycling do virtually no damage to the environment.**

- **It's safer to walk or cycle with a group of friends – and it's more fun too!**

- **Ask your school to provide safe places to leave bikes and cycle helmets.**

- **Car share whenever you can.**

Ask each member of your family to cut their car journeys – get them to sign this pledge below.

I pledge to stop travelling by car for _____ days each week.

Yes – on _____ days out of seven I won't rely on cars to cart me around.

That's my contribution to cut traffic pollution – guaranteed!

Signed_____

(Photocopy this pledge so that all the members of your family can sign it)

Mum and Dad, and other relatives may need an incentive to go that extra mile without wheels. But if you promise to reward their efforts they can hardly refuse, can they?

TO WHOM IT CONCERNS

I promise to

_____

(eg walk to the shop to buy my newspaper/let the train take the strain when we next visit Auntie Mabel, etc)

Signed _____

(Mum/Dad/Main car potato in household fills in this bit)

I promise that if

_____

curbs his/her use of the car, I'll

_____

_____

_____

(eg Bring Dad a cup of tea every morning for a term, let Mum watch what ever she likes on telly – whenever she likes! etc)

Now, how's that for a bargain?

Signed _____

(You fill in this bit)

If your school is too far way to walk, and there's REALLY no bus or train going that way, then club together with your friends to set up a car sharing scheme for the school run.

Car sharing reduces road traffic, saves petrol and gives parents more free time! The rota printed below will help you get going. The scheme stands more chance of success if you can get parents to commit to the same mornings and afternoons every week.

		MORNING	AFTERNOON
MON	D		
	P		
TUE	D		
	P		
WED	D		
	P		
THU	D		
	P		
FRI	D		
	P		

D=DRIVER P=PASSENGERS

Encourage others to share cars: eg parents and teachers. Stick up posters at school or youth club to match up people who regularly travel the same way. Ask your teachers to record their car use over a week (photocopy the form on page 93).* Hand out parking tickets to teachers who over use their cars. Here's one we made earlier.

You're a car potato and a greedy gas guzzler! And you're BOOKED!

- Do your homework! Find out how you can travel to school without your car.
- And pledge to leave your car at home whenever you can.

Because if you don't, you'll be driving yourself to a detention!

BY ORDER

signed_____
(a real fresh air fiend!)

Ask the teacher to justify why they drove in on certain days. Turn the tables on your teachers. If they say "*Erm, I didn't have time this morning*", you can tactfully ask what they would think if you "*didn't have time*" to do your homework.

*Extra keen greenies might also like to check how many of their teachers' car journeys could have been made by bus, train or tram by finding out about public transport in the area.

CAMPAIGNING IDEAS

Campaign for traffic reduction in your area. Ask each member of your group to collect statements from ten people confirming that they would leave their cars at home two days a week if public transport better. Then present these statements to the Council. Invite the local media to photograph the presentation. If you can give them a good picture opportunity they are more likely to turn up.

Start a petition to improve public transport and cycle facilities in your area. Demand better bus services, more cycle lanes and plenty of safe places to park your bike in town. Send it to the Council – and the media.

Find out whether any roads are being built or widened in your area. Start a petition to stop any unnecessary road schemes. The Department of Transport has abandoned road-buildling plans before in the face of local campaigns. For example the planned highway through ancient Oxleas Wood in South London was ditched, thanks to campaigning from local people, Friends of the Earth and other organisations.

ARE YOU A FRESH AIR FIEND
OR A GREEDY GAS GUZZLER?

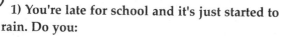

Try our quick quiz and find out

1) You're late for school and it's just started to rain. Do you:

   a) Come over all poorly and spend the day at home watching TV?

   b) Pretend you've got a maths exam so that mum or dad carts you there by car?

   c) Pull on your cycle cape and start pedalling - better late than never?

2) Your next door neighbour, Simon Spoilt, is given a sports car for his 17th birthday. Do you:

a) Turn green with envy and hope he gets a puncture?

b) Pretend to be interested even though you'd be more impressed by a 21-gear mountain bike?

c) Hope it's got a catalytic converter - sports cars really burn up petrol?

3) Your pals point out that you're a bit unfit. Do you:

   a) Throw away the TV zapper. Getting up to change channels should work off some weight?

   b) Start getting up extra early to walk to school?

   c) Offer to run errands for mum and dad on your bike - providing they bump up your pocket money!

4) There's a group outing to Alton Towers and you're in charge of the travel arrangements. Do you:

a) Book a place for everyone with a local bus company; coach travel is cheaper and saves energy!

b) Persuade a few parents to take everyone in a car convoy, even though the gig is 50 miles away.

c) Book a minibus –with seat belts of course!

HOW TO SCORE			
1)	a) 2	b) 1	c) 3
2)	a) 1	b) 2	c) 3
3)	a) 1	b) 3	c) 2
4)	a) 3	b) 1	c) 2

WELL, HOW DID YOU DO?

9-12 Crikey, you really are a fresh-air fiend! You'll go to any lengths to avoid using cars – and persuade your parents and pals to cut their car use too. And you've done your homework – you know why overusing cars is so harmful to the environment. You're a car-conscious, smog buster – keep it up!

5-8 Hmmm. You're no stranger to public tranport and you rate bikes over cars. But when it comes to the crunch you can be a tad lazy – you could do with cycling or bus-ing it more often. Why not try walking with friends whenever you can? That way you'll save money, and stay safe and healthy.

0-4 Embarassing or what? You're a greedy gas guzzler and no mistake. In fact you're only happy travelling on four wheels. 'Car potatoes' like you are in danger of getting heart disease in later life. So now is the time to get on your bike, become a Friend of the Earth and pedal for a brighter future!

Chapter Ten

OFF YOUR TROLLEY

Everything we buy has some impact on the environment – but some products are worse than others.

They may be wastefully wrapped or have guzzled up gallons of polluting fumes being packed and delivered to the shelf.

Animals might have suffered making them, or people exploited – workers in some countries are paid little and live very poorly.

As you read through this chapter you'll find lots to be angry about the way the world's markets work. Let's start by looking at how supermarkets play a part in all this...

SUPERMARKETS – NOT SO SUPER AFTER ALL!

A trolley full of tasty treats may come cheap at the local supermarket. But the environment is paying for the savings we're making.

Supermarkets built on the outskirts of towns and cities can destroy valuable countryside. 100 new superstores are built every year. Each one takes up just over three hectares of land for the store itself, and the supply roads and other facilities. That's as much as four and a half football pitches!

Supermarkets take business away from neighbourhood shops and encourage car travel. Superstore shoppers almost all travel by car. A recent survey at Asda near High Wycombe found that of 236 customers interviewed, only four did not come by car!

FOOD MILES

It takes up to four litres of fuel to carry just one kilo of fruit and vegetables from California to Europe.

The shelves of UK supermarkets are piled high with tempting goodies from across the globe all year round. Even if a fruit or vegetable isn't in season over here you'll be able to buy it locally. For example, in the UK we can grow strawberries, plums and lettuces in summer only. But browse round the fruit and vegetable counters of a big supermarket in winter and you'll find strawberries from South America, plums from Africa and leafy greens from the USA. Before you put them in your basket, think about the pollution caused by delivering these foods to our doorsteps.

Bag Gripes

Not so very long ago, shoppers relied on sturdy wicker baskets or canvas bags to carry their shopping home. Today's customers tend to use carrier bags given away free at supermarkets and other shops – at the Earth's expense.

Sainsbury's 'penny-back' scheme encourages shoppers to reuse their carriers. This is said to be saving 1 million bags, 20,000 gallons of oil and 20 tonnes of plastic every week! Think how much more could be saved if every shop did this.

- If your supermarket isn't encouraging its customers to reuse carrier bags, it's time to persuade them to. Collect as many of their plastic bags as possible – ask your friends and family to help. When you've amassed a monster collection make an appointment with the supermarket manager so that you can return the bags to him/her in person. Explain that supermarkets must help stop their policy of 'one-trip' packaging.

Improve your green power by reusing carrier bags – or refusing them in the first place. Cut out the sticker below and glue it to your purse as a reminder.

Be a super sleuth. When you next help mum/dad with the weekly shop check out what's on offer. Track down products which do as little harm to the environment as possible. Make a list of your favourite 'green' products and/or shops for future reference.

My favourite cruelty-free shampoo is

_____

I'd prefer mum/dad to wash my clothes in

_____

_____

I can buy a whole range of organic vegetables at

_____

The best energy-efficient device I've ever bought is

_____

_____

I can buy ace recycled file paper for school at

_____

What you can do

- Do your own customer survey while you're waiting at the checkout. Ask the other shoppers in your queue how far they have travelled and how they made the journey there?

- Help your local community – support your local shops. These might charge a little more for some products but they save you time and the costs of travelling to out-of-town supermarket sites.

- Examine a week's worth of food items and find out which country produced them. How many different countries of origin can you see? Could any of the produce have been grown locally?

- Persuade your parents to buy locally produced goods.

- Do our supermarket survey (see page 116).

GREEN CONS – DON'T BE FOOLED

When out shopping choose products that can be Re-used, Refilled or Recycled – for maximum purse power! You can Reduce waste by always buying products with as little packaging as possible.

Unfortunately making the right choice is easier said than done. Manufacturers know that shoppers feel good buying 'green' products. Some claim in big type how environmentally friendly their products are. But beware – you could be being conned!

Don't let them get away with it – keep an eye out for:

- **Recycled paper loo rolls.** These sound like a good idea but in fact a lot of recycled loo roll is made from high-grade waste paper which could be turned into something of higher quality such as writing paper. Always buy low-grade paper loo rolls – they're made from old newspapers and magazines.

- **Washing powder packets** with 'environmental information' such as *"Biodegradable – breaks down in the environment"*. All detergents have to be at least 80 per cent biodegradable within 19 days by law.

- **"This packaging can be recycled".** Keen greenies know that most packaging could be recycled. But unless people make the effort to take do so, it won't be! Sometimes, even if you want to recycle something, there may not be facilities near you to do so. You're better off buying a similar product which comes in recycled or refillable packaging.

If you spot any of the green cons mentioned above, pour shame on the guilty parties. Fill in and cut out the Green Con Award opposite, and then pop it in the post. If you don't want to cut up this book you can photocopy the page, or, better still, make your own award. You could do this as part of a school project. After all, the more awards manufacturers receive, the more likely they are to change their ways.

WARNING!

Paper products often carry misleading messages about 'sustainable forestry'. This usually means 'factory forests', dense plantations of little value for wildlife or local inhabitants. Buy recycled paper instead.

Dear ......

_____

(write manufacturer's name here)

You've been telling a few fibs on the packaging of

_____

(Write the name of the product)

But you can't fool me. I know your product is not so green as it seems because

_____

(Fill in the reason why you feel their claim is exaggerated/not strictly true/an outrageous lie!)

Please accept this green con award from me. I won't be buying your product again until you stop misleading shoppers.

Signed _____

Name _____

Address_____

_____

GREEN CON AWARD

ANIMAL MATTERS

Whether you're a meat eater or not, you must have noticed that most people expect meat as a daily part of their diet, although this never used to be the case. When your grandparents were young, meat was a Sunday treat. Today, however, school canteens and fast food restaurants are bulging with beef burgers, chicken nuggets, and turkey bites – at the planet's expense.

To satisfy our increased appetite for meat and animal products, many farms at home and abroad are rearing animals very unnaturally. This means keeping animals in cruel conditions. For example, cows which naturally graze on grass are now being kept in sheds and forced to eat special food that contains meat! And chickens are kept in very small spaces. This is called intensive farming.

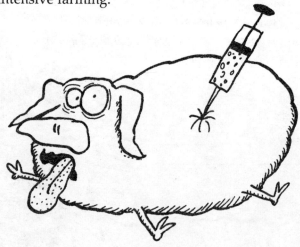

More food for thought:
30 million hens are kept in cages about as big as a page of your favourite comic. These are called battery cages.

In the UK we rear and kill 600 million broiler chickens each year. Think how many tonnes of polluting waste 600 million chickens make.

Some animals are kept for all their lives in dark, stinky sheds and are fed large doses of antibiotics and chemicals to keep them alive and growing.

Pricey *foie gras paté* is a very posh food. It is made from the fatty livers of forcefed ducks. It has been estimated that nearly 2 million children could be fed on the grain used to produce 200 tonnes of *foie gras*.

But it's not only animals that are being farmed intensively. Today, our crops are farmed this way too.

Tonnes of bug-zapping pesticides are sprayed onto crops, and soils are soaked with fertiliser to bump up the crop. This kills off butterflies, birds and flowers, and can damage our health too.

Some pesticides get absorbed by plants and then by the animals that feed on them. Animals at the top of food chains such as herons and otters – and humans – can accumulate dangerously high levels of pesticides inside their bodies. By law most farmers have to spray or paint strong chemicals on to farm animals' coats to keep bugs at bay. But these are so strong they can make the farmers ill.

WHAT IS ORGANIC FARMING?

Some farmers in Britain are producing food without using modern artificial fertilisers, weed-killers and pesticides. This is called organic farming. It is good because it reduces river pollution and that means fewer problems for us all.

OVER TO YOU

✎ Write to your MP asking him/her to try to persuade the Government to ban battery hen farming.

🚩 Eat more locally grown vegetables instead of meat. (Beware of soya products – they're imported from the other side of the world and so guzzle up lots of food miles!)

🚩 Don't buy meat that has been intensively farmed. Choose free-range or organic meat instead. If you don't agree with eating meat you can be a vegetarian and still be perfectly healthy. Contact VIVA! (Vegetarians International Voice for Animals) for advice and encouragement.

🚩 Find out from the Soil Association where you can buy locally-produced organic vegetables and meat. Look for the Soil Association symbol. It is awarded to producers who do not use dangerous chemicals or intensive farming.

If you're wild about animals and against animal testing always buy cruelty-free products.

WHY SOME COUNTRIES ARE BETTER OFF THAN OTHERS

At the moment, the world is anything but fair. The richest quarter of the world's population uses over half of the world's energy, three-quarters of its metals, and two-thirds of its food.

The richer countries, such as the UK, the US and Japan, have a lot of power over poorer 'developing' countries. They often use this to their own advantage rather than helping other countries to develop sustainably. Even the aid money governments give doesn't always help. A great deal of aid money from rich countries to poor ones is given directly to their governments or even to big companies. The poorest people don't always get it.

Not many farmers in 'developing' countries receive a fair price for the things they sell. The richest countries control the price of things around the world, and keep lots of the profits for themselves.

African countries are only able to pay about one third of the interest due on their debts. Even this is more than everything they spend on the health and education of their own people.

Press for change by buying more products which have been 'fairly traded'. Fair trade means paying the producers a decent wage and not destroying their environment. Look out for 'fair trade' coffee, tea and chocolate (and tell your mum or dad to do the same). Fair trade products carry the symbol shown below.

Fairtrade

ACTION POINTS

Write to your MP if you think governments could do more to help poorer countries. Ask him or her to press for more aid money to be targeted at the poorest countries and designed specifically to help stop poverty.

SUPERMARKET SWEEP!

You can help the people who own supermarkets to take responsibility for what their business does to the planet. Find out which of your local supermarkets and other shops has the greenest policy, and support them.

Why not use the letter opposite as your starting point. Write it out yourself in your neatest handwriting – or better still, type it. If you haven't received a reply within a month, write again. Write to your local newspaper with your survey results, challenging the supermarkets to do better.

And remember these three steps to ecofriendly shopping:

1) Buy food from local farmers.

2) Walk to the shops, or go by bike, bus, tube, train or tram.

3) If you have a choice, buy things in materials you can recycle locally. Don't buy overpackaged products.

4) Buy things that can be reused – time and time again.

5) Before you buy something, stop and ask how long it will last. If it breaks or wears out, can it be easily repaired?

Dear Sir

I am concerned about the environment and want to help
protect our planet. I want to be a green consumer but
I need your help.

I would be most grateful if you could take time to
answer a few questions about your company's
environmental policies.

Please tell me:
- whether you stock
- organic produce?
- fair trade produce ?
- locally grown produce?
- recycled paper products eg toilet
  paper/tissues?
- green cleaning products - and can you
  explain why these products are green?
(beware of green cons and vague claims)
- what efforts your firm has made to reduce
packaging?
- if there are recycling banks on your
  premises?
- if you operate refillable bottle schemes?
- if you recycle your in-store waste?
- if your refrigeration is free of
  ozone-damaging chemicals?
- what measures the company has taken to
  conserve energy?
- what your company policy is on developing
out-of-town sites?
- what you do to make it easy for people to
reach the supermarket by bike or public
transport?

I look forward to hearing from you soon

Yours faithfully

What you decide to buy when you shop can change the world. Big supermarkets only put things on their shelves that they can sell. So by using your purse power and refusing to buy eco-unfriendly products you can force supermarkets to replace them with ones that are better for the planet.

Don't forget, the more you, and your family, use your purse power, the easier it will be for everyone to be green!

Your weekly shop doesn't need to cost the Earth. Snip out our good buys shopping list opposite and give it to the main shopper in your household. Ask friends' parents if they'd like one too.

SUPER SHOPPER LIST FOR PARENTS

Good buys:
- ✔ free-range eggs
- ✔ organic meat, fruit and veg
- ✔ products which haven't been tested on animals
- ✔ recycled paper
- ✔ products which come in reusable or recyclable packaging
- ✔ fair trade foods
- ✔ organically grown produce
- ✔ energy-efficient lightbulbs
- ✔ pump-action sprays (instead of aerosols)
- ✔ the most energy-efficient washing machines, ghetto blasters etc
- ✔ rechargable batteries

ARE YOU A SUPER-EARTHSAVER OR A REAL BIG SPENDER?

Try this quick quiz and find out

1) **It's tuna for tea and Mum's sent you to the corner shop to buy some. Do you:**
a) come back with a couple of cans – one for tea and one for tomorrow's packed lunch?
b) check all the cans on sale and plump for a dolphin-friendly brand?
c) buy a tin of sweetcorn instead? Even dolphin-friendly tuna isn't tuna-friendly enough for your liking!

2) **It's mum's birthday. Your idea of the perfect present is:**
a) a bunch of flowers – and the bigger, the better?
b) some swanky perfume – in a refillable pump-action sprayer, of course?
c) some cruelty-free bath oil and a bar of 'fairly-traded' chocolate? Mum's a friend of the Earth too!

3) **When you go shopping do you ever:**
(you may tick more than one box)
a) cadge a lift in a friend's car?
b) go by bus or another form of public transport?
c) go by bike?
d) Walk?

4) It's your turn to help your parents do the weekly shop. At the supermarket checkout, do you:

a) quickly stuff everything you've bought into the shop's own placcy bags, though you suspect they'll split on the way home?

b) proudly pop all your goodies into that wheelie-basket you borrowed from gran!

c) ask the manager to find you a cardboard box – after all, the shop must have loads going spare!

HOW TO SCORE

1)	a) 1	b) 2	c) 3
2)	a) 1	b) 2	c) 3
3) score one point for every box ticked			
4)	a) 1	b) 3	c) 2

WELL, JUST HOW GREEN ARE YOU THEN?

9-13 Wow, you really know how to use your purse power! You enjoy refusing unwanted bags, reusing packaging when possible and collecting stuff to recycle. You're passionate about animal cruelty too. And you don't need a car to get you places. You're a full-on eco warrior.

4-8 You're well on your way to becoming a super-Earthsaver. You've read up on the planet's problems, you know about ways you can help and you try to stick to them. Keep up the good work.

0-3 Uh-oh! You're a real big spender and it's the poor old planet that's paying for it. Wake up and smell the coffee. And reread the whole of chapter ten again!

HOT CONTACTS

House of Commons
London SW1A 0AA
Tel: 0171 219 4272 - info
Tel: 0171 219 3000 - MPs

House of Lords
London SW1A 0PW
Tel: 0171 219 3107 - info
Tel: 0171 219 3000 - Lords

GOVERNMENT DEPARTMENTS AND AGENCIES

Department of the Environment
2 Marsham Street
London SW1P 3EB
Tel: 0171 276 3000

Department of the Environment Northern Ireland
Environment & Heritage Service
Commonwealth House
35 Castle Street
Belfast BT1 1GU
Tel: 01232 251477

Department of the Environment Ireland
Custom House
Dublin 1
Tel: 01 679 3377

Department of Trade and Industry Environment Unit
151 Buckingham Palace Road
London SW1W 9SS
Tel: 0800 585 794

Department of Transport
2 Marsham Street
London SW1P 3EB
Tel: 0171 276 5089

Ministry of Agriculture, Fisheries and Food (MAFF)
Whitehall Place
London SW1A 2HH
Tel: 0171 270 3000

Overseas Development Adminstration
94 Victoria Street
London SW1E 5JL
Tel: 0171 917 0503/0950

English Nature
Northminster House
Northminster Road
Peterborough
Cambridgeshire PE1 1UA
Tel: 01733 340345

Countryside Council for Wales
Plas Penrhos
Ffordd Penrhos
Bangor
Gwynedd LL57 2LQ
Tel: 01248 37044

Scottish Natural Heritage
12 Hope Terrace
Edinburgh EH9 2AS
Tel: 0131 447 4784

The Environment Agency
Rivers House
Waterside Drive
Aztec West
Almondsbury
Bristol BS14 4UD

Scottish Environment Agency
Saughton House
Suite VI
Broom House Drive
Edinburgh EH11 3XD

European Commission
8 Storey's Gate
London SW1P 3AT
Tel: 0171 973 1992

NON-GOVERNMENT ORGANISATIONS

Friends of the Earth
(England, Wales & Northern Ireland)
26-28 Underwood Street
London N1 7JQ
Tel: 0171 490 1555
Fax: 0171 490 0881

Friends of the Earth Scotland
Bonnington Mill
72 Newhaven Rd
Edinburgh EH6 5QG
Tel: 0131 554 9977
Fax: 0131 554 8656

Friends of the Earth Ireland
(Earthwatch)
Harbour View
Bantry
Cork
Tel: 027 50968
Fax:: 027 50545

Friends of the Earth International
Prins Hendrikkade 48
Room 27
1012 AC Amsterdam
Netherlands
Tel: 00 31 20 622 1369
Fax: 00 31 20 639 2181

ALARM UK
(Alliance Against Roadbuilding)
Southbank House
Black Prince Road
London SE1 7SJ
Tel: 0171 582 9279

**British Trust for
Conservation Volunteeers
(BTCV)**
36 St Mary's Street
Wallingford
Oxon OX10 0EU
Tel: 01491 839766
Fax: 01491 839646

**Centre for Alternative
Technology**
Llwyngwern Quarry
Machynlleth
Powys SY20 9AZ
Tel: 01654 702400
Fax: 01654 702782

Cyclists Campaign Network
c/o London Cycling Campaign
Tress House
3 Stamford Street
London SE1 9NT
Tel: 0171 928 7220

Food Commission
3rd Floor
5-11 Worship St
London EC2A 2BH
Tel: 0171 628 7774

Greenpeace
Greenpeace House
Canonbury Villas
London N1 2PN
Tel: 0171 354 5100
Fax: 0171 696 0013

League Against Cruel Sports
83-87 Union Street
London SE1 1SG
Tel: 0171 403 6155

Marine Conservation Society
9 Gloucester Road
Ross-on-Wye
Herefordshire HR9 5BU
Tel: 01989 566017
Fax: 01989 567815

We're FRIENDS of the EARTH

Oxfam
274 Banbury Road
Oxford OX2 7DZ
Tel: 01865 311311
Fax: 01865 57612

Pedestrians Association
126 Aldersgate Rd
London EC1 4JQ
Tel: 0171 490 0750

**People for the Ethical
Treatment of Animals (PETA)**
PO Box 3169
London NW1 2JF
Tel: 0171 388 4922
Fax: 0171 388 4925

Population Concern
178-202 Great Portland Street
London W1N 5TB
Tel: 0171 637 9582

**Royal Society for the
Protection of Birds (RSPB)**
The Lodge
Sandy
Beds SG19 2DL
Tel: 01767 680 551
Fax: 01767 692 365
RSPB Scotland
17 Regent Terrace
Edinburgh
EH7 5BN
Tel: 0131 557 3136

Soil Association
(promotes organic farming)
86-88 Colston Street
Bristol BS1 5BB
Tel: 0117 290661
Fax: 0117 252504

Surfers Against Sewage
The Old Country House
Wheal Kitty
St Agnes
Cornwall
TR5 0RE
Tel: 01872 553001
Fax: 01872 552615

RECYCLE ME!

**Sustrans (Sustainable
Transport)**
35 King Street
Bristol BS1 4DZ
Tel: 0117 926 8893

Tourism Concern
Southlands College
Roehampton Institute
Wimbledon Parkside
London SW19 5NN
Tel: 0181 944-0464

Urban Wildlife Trust
Unit 310, Jubilee Trades Centre
130 Pershore St
Birmingham B5 6ND
Tel: 0121 666 7474

Viva!
(Vegetarians International Voice
for Animals)
PO Box 212
Crewe
Cheshire CW1 4SD
Tel: 01270 522500
Fax: 01270 522511

Waste Watch
(recycling information)
Gresham House
24 Holbern Viaduct
London EC1A 2BN
Tel: 0171 248 0242
Fax: 0171 248 1404

**Whale and Dolphin
Conservation Society**
Alexander House
James St West
Bath
Avon BA1 2BT
Tel: 01225 334511

Wildlife Trusts (a nationwide
network)
The Green
Witham Park
Waterside South
Lincoln LN5 7JR
Tel: 01522
Fax: 01522 511616

Woodcraft Folk
13 Ritherdon Road
London SW17 8QE
Tel: 0181 672 60131
Fax: 0181 767 2457

**World Wide Fund for Nature
(WWF)**
Panda House
Weyside Park
Godalming
Surrey GU7 1XR
Tel: 01483 426444
Fax: 01483 426409

WWF Scotland
1 Crieff Road
Aberfeldy
Perthshire
PH15 2BJ
Tel: 01887 820449
Fax: 01887 829453

Zoo Check
Cherry Tree Cottage
Coldharbour
Dorking
Surrey RH5 6HA
Tel: 01306 712091

BOOST YOUR PESTER POWER - JOIN FRIENDS OF THE EARTH AND REALLY GET RESULTS!

If you're under 18, you can join Friends of the Earth for only £8 a year!

The more people who join us the more we can do to fight environmental destruction.

If you join you'll receive a copy of our magazine Earth Matters, four times a year. It has a brilliant pull out section for young people called Kids Matters which is packed with info, your news and views, competitions and tonnes of ideas for how you can protect the planet.

Just fill in the coupon below and send it to us together with a postal order or cheque from your parents made payable to Friends of the Earth.

Yes! There's no time to lose. Please make me a member of Friends of the Earth NOW!

My name_____

My address_____

_____

_____Postcode_____

I enclose a cheque/postal order made payable to Friends of the Earth for £8

☐ Please send me information about Friends of the Earth's youth campaign. PB95095297

☐ Please send me your catalogue of children's books and leaflets'.

Cut out or photocopy this form and send it to:
Friends of the Earth
FREEPOST
56-58 Alma Street
Luton
Beds LU1 2YZ

No stamp needed, but your stamp will help save us money.
You can also join by credit card, phone 01582 482297